The life of
Malala Yousafzai

I am Malala Yousafzai. I am an activist for girls' education. Where I grew up many people believed that girls shouldn't go to school. Luckily for me my mother and father believed all children should have the same opportunities. They encouraged me to learn and to speak out against injustices.

However, one day when I was 15 years old, I was shot, along with two school friends, on the bus on our way home from school. The Taliban, a violent group of extremists who wanted to stop girls from learning and to take away women's rights, tried to silence me with a bullet. Come along as I share the story of my incredible journey from being the girl who was shot to the girl who stood up for justice for other girls.

I was born on July 12, 1997, in Mingora, a city in the northwest of Pakistan, in the beautiful Swat Valley. I was very happy living there among the snow-topped mountains, lush green hills, sparkling waterfalls, and crystal-clear rivers.

I have two younger brothers, Khushal and Atal. As children, we argued a lot (and still do now!) but we loved playing together. When I wasn't busy studying my books, or daydreaming about how I could make the world a better place, I would go outside and play hide-and-seek and cricket with my brothers and our neighbors. Our family didn't have much money but we had a happy home full of love and laughter.

My father, Ziauddin, was a teacher, and he ran his own schools for boys and girls. Unlike many Pashtun men, he believed girls and women should be given the same opportunities and respect as boys and men. And he believed that quality education for all was the key to making this happen. He was, and continues to be, my inspiration to fight against injustices in the world.

My mother, Toor Pekai, like many girls of her generation, didn't go to school for long, but she always encouraged me to study and work hard at school. She shared my father's passion for education for all and helped him run his schools. And she always supported my father and me when we gave interviews to raise awareness about the terrible things that were happening in our country.

From a very young age I began to be aware that women and men were treated differently in our society. It was traditional for girls to be married off at a young age, and many fathers didn't send their daughters to school because they thought they didn't need an education to run their husband's household.

Many women stayed at home, doing all the cooking and cleaning. They covered their faces when they went out, and they could only speak to men that were their relatives. This made me feel sad and confused. I didn't want my life to be like this when I grew up, and I wondered if there was a way to change this.

When I talked to my father about my worries, he told me that things were even worse for women in Afghanistan, the country next to ours, where a group called the Taliban had taken over. They had burned down schools for girls and had forced women to wear a garment that covered them from head to toe with only a tiny fabric grill over their eyes so that they could see. If women went out for a walk without a male relative they would be beaten or put in jail.

This was the first time I had heard about the Taliban, and I was shocked by what they were doing. My father told me not to worry and that he would protect my freedom. He told me to carry on with my big dreams for a better world. I didn't know at that time that there were also Taliban groups in Pakistan and that it wouldn't be long before their extreme beliefs about women would begin to affect my happy childhood.

For a while life was still good. I was at my father's school learning everything I could and competing with my friends for top grades. By the time I was eight years old my father had set up several schools and had more than 800 students. We were able to afford to buy a TV, and I spent some of my spare time watching my favorite shows.

There was one show where a boy had a magic pencil. He could make anything real just by drawing it. I had seen children my age digging through the garbage dumps in our city to find metal and glass to sell to make some money for their families. They couldn't go to school because they had to work. I longed to have a magic pencil of my own so that I could change things and all children could go to school like me.

In 2005, the same year I realized that it would take more than a magic pencil to make changes and that carrying on with my education was the best way I could help people, a huge earthquake hit the Swat Valley. Many buildings collapsed in my city, and in some areas whole villages were destroyed, along with thousands of schools. Over a million people lost their homes.

The government of Pakistan did very little to help the people whose lives had been destroyed by the earthquake. This lack of action allowed extreme groups, like the Taliban, to rise to power. They offered aid to win people over, at the same time telling them that the earthquake was a punishment from God because they were not properly following Islamic law.

I am Muslim, and my family and I practice the religion of Islam, which was founded by the Prophet Muhammad. We pray to God, whom we call Allah, and follow our holy book, which is called the Qur'an. The Qur'an is the collection of messages that Muhammad received from Allah.

The Taliban are also Muslim, but their extreme beliefs misrepresent the Islamic faith. They believe that women should not be educated, should stay at home and be silent, and don't have any rights or freedoms. They say that this is what's written in the Qur'an, but that isn't true. Islam teaches that men and women are equal before God.

In my country a lot of people couldn't read or write, so they didn't know what was really written in the Qur'an. The Taliban took advantage of this fact and told them that the earthquake happened because women had too many freedoms. Many people began to believe this, and over the next few years, the Taliban continued to spread their anti-women message.

When I was 10 years old, a Taliban leader named Maulana Fazlullah started a radio station, which he used to spread his message against women's freedoms. His followers started burning and smashing TVs, computers, DVDs, CDs, and books and also destroyed schools, blaming these things for leading people astray. Fazlullah announced that girls should not go to school.

It was a frightening time. My father said we should not do what Fazlullah was telling us. He wanted to stop the Taliban. He kept his schools open, encouraging students to speak out against the extremists. I carried on going to school, hiding my books under my shawl as I walked to class.

It was becoming increasingly difficult to ignore what was happening around us. People were afraid to speak out, and so they started going along with what the Taliban wanted. With my father's encouragement, I became an activist like him. I knew what was happening in my country was wrong, and I couldn't stay quiet and watch the Taliban destroy the lives of millions of girls and women, and my future.

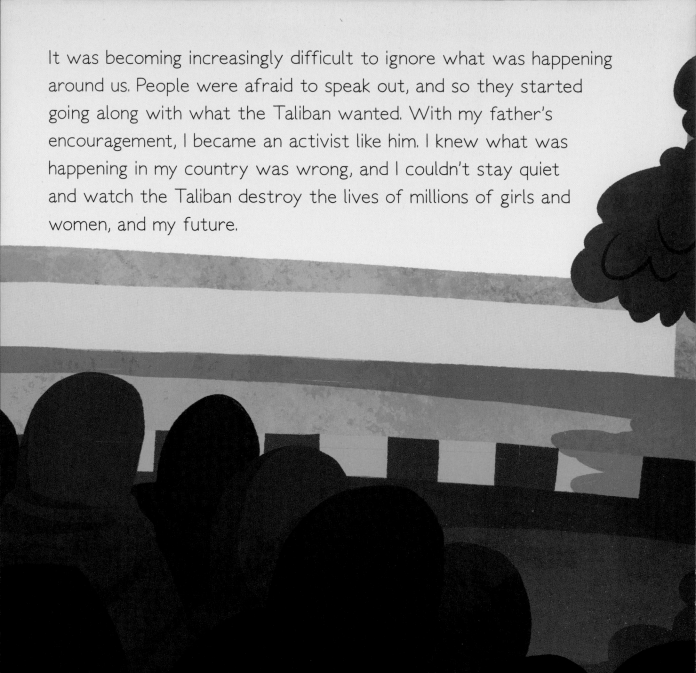

Although it was dangerous, I started giving interviews, going to rallies, and giving speeches about the importance of education, especially for girls. I gave my first public speech in September 2008, titled "How Dare the Taliban Take Away My Basic Right to Education?"

In 2009, Fazlullah shut down all girls' schools in the Swat Valley and said that girls over 10 years old were no longer allowed to attend school. I was nearly 12 years old, but of course I was not going to let this stop me. I carried on going to school in secret and continued speaking out against the Taliban.

That same year, I started a blog about my experiences as a schoolgirl under the Taliban for the BBC's Urdu language website. I had to use a false name, Gul Makai, to hide my identity. My father and I were already getting threats to our safety from the Taliban.

Pakistan's government eventually sent in the army to try and clear out the Taliban. This meant most of the people living in the Swat Valley were forced to leave their homes. My family and I stayed with relatives until we could return to Mingora. When we returned three months later, I was able to go back to school, but the Taliban were still a threat.

I was determined to carry on fighting for girls' rights to an education. I knew that words could be powerful, and my voice was beginning to be heard around the world. At the age of 14, I was awarded two prizes for my campaigning: the first Pakistan National Youth Peace Prize and the International Children's Peace Prize. I used the prize money to help schools and street children in Pakistan.

By the time I was 15, the threats against me from the Taliban had increased, and my family was very concerned for my safety. I was worried, too, but I had promised myself to stay calm and carry on. I felt I was stronger than fear. The day of October 9, 2012, started out like any other day. I went to school to take an exam.

As usual I took the school bus home with my friends. That is when everything changed. Two men boarded our bus and asked which of us was Malala. I don't remember anything after that. I had been shot in the head, and two of my school friends were also shot and injured.

I nearly died that day, but I was fortunate that the doctors in charge of my care were able to fly me to a special hospital in Birmingham, England, and they saved my life. After lots of operations and rehabilitation treatments I was eventually allowed to leave the hospital in January 2013.

Because I had dared to speak out against the Taliban, I could not return home to Pakistan. This made me very sad, but my family came to Birmingham, and we started our new lives together as I slowly recovered from my injuries.

Going to school in England was a new and strange experience for me. I missed my friends from home, especially my best friend Moniba, but I made lots of new friends. I studied hard, and when I finished secondary school, or high school, I was able to go to Oxford University to study politics, philosophy, and economics. Alongside this, I continued my campaign for girls' education, traveling around the world to deliver my message, writing books, and appearing on TV.

The Taliban had tried to silence me with a bullet, but instead their actions had the opposite effect. People all over the world knew my name and wanted to support my cause. Instead of only my voice, there were now thousands of voices shouting loudly for change and equality for women and girls.

When I was little I had wanted to be a doctor, but now I knew what
I had to do. I had become an international symbol for the fight for girls'
education, and I wanted to continue this work. On my 16th birthday I got
to speak at the United Nations, where I called for free education for
all children. My father and I set up the Malala Fund that year to bring
awareness to the social and economic impact of girls' education and to
help empower girls everywhere to demand change for themselves and
to tackle social injustice.

I have been fortunate to receive several awards and prizes in recognition of my work. In 2014, I became the youngest person in the world to win the Nobel Peace Prize, along with children's rights activist Kailash Satyarthi. I use any prize money I win to open schools for girls in the places they are most needed.

When someone takes away your pencils, you realize how important education is. I know there is still a lot more work to do, but my goal is to bring education and equality to girls all around the world. Many things like war, poverty, child labor, early marriage, and gender discrimination threaten a girl's education, so the world must find a way to ensure that every girl can complete 12 years of free, safe, and quality education.

This is my mission. Remember, always dream big and don't be afraid to speak out for what is right.

The Afghan Taliban take control of Kabul, the capital of Afghanistan, after years of civil war.

Malala's brother Khushal is born.

Malala's brother Atal is born.

1996

1997

2000

2001

2004

Malala is born.

Terrorists hijack and crash planes into the World Trade Center towers in New York City. The United States begins bombing Afghanistan, and the Taliban government is overthrown.

In September, Malala gives her first public speech in Peshawar, against the Taliban and about the importance of education, titled "How Dare the Taliban Take Away My Basic Right to Education?"

In October, Malala wins the International Children's Peace Prize. In December, she wins the first Pakistan National Youth Peace Prize.

2008

2011

2005

2009

2012

The Swat Valley is hit by one of its biggest earthquakes in October.

Malala and two of her school friends are shot by the Taliban on the bus home from school.

Malala writes her first blog entry ("I Am Afraid") as Gul Makai, for the BBC's Urdu website.

Malala speaks at the United Nations on her 16th birthday. She calls for free education for all children. The UN declares July 12 as Malala Day.

Malala wins the Nobel Peace Prize, sharing it with children's rights activist Kailash Satyarthi.

2013

2014

2013

2015

In October, Malala's biography, *I Am Malala: The Girl Who Stood Up for Education and Was Shot by the Taliban*, is published, and Malala and her father set up the Malala Fund.

In April, the Malala Fund launches a campaign to give every child around the world the right to a minimum of 12 years of education. Malala asks world leaders to promise they will ensure that all children will have access to quality education by 2030.

Malala starts attending
Oxford University.

Malala marries Asser Malik.

2017

2021

2020

2022

Malala graduates from
Oxford University.

Malala receives the LionHeart
Award, which honors people
who have used their position
to make a positive change
in the world.

QUESTIONS

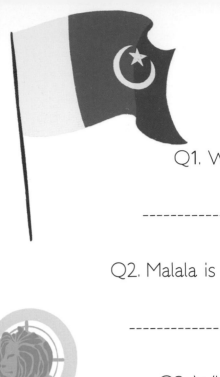

Q1. When and where was Malala born?

Q2. Malala is an activist. What does she campaign for?

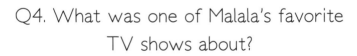

Q3. What job did Malala's father do before
he went to England?

Q4. What was one of Malala's favorite
TV shows about?

Q5. Who started a radio station when
Malala was 10 to spread his message
against women's freedoms?

Q6. What year did Malala give her first public speech and what was it about?

Q7. Who threatened and shot Malala and where was she when it happened?

Q8. Where did Malala give a speech on her 16th birthday?

Q9. In 2014, Malala was the youngest person in the world to do what?

Q10. What does the Malala Fund do?

ANSWERS

A1. July 12, 1997, in Mingora, Swat Valley, in Pakistan.

A2. Education for all, in particular for girls.

A3. He was a teacher. He ran schools for boys and girls.

A4. A boy who had a magic pencil.

A5. A Taliban leader named Maulana Fazlullah.

A6. In 2008. It was titled *"How Dare the Taliban Take Away My Basic Right to Education?"*

A7. The Taliban. Malala and two of her school friends were shot on the school bus on their way home.

A8. The United Nations.

A9. Win the Nobel Peace Prize.

A10. The Malala Fund is an organization that raises funds for and brings awareness to the impact of girls' education, helping to empower girls everywhere to demand change for themselves.